Strategies and Activities for Building Literacy

*For Teachers & Students
Who Are Growing
in Whole Language*

by Karen Grindall

SCHOLASTIC
PROFESSIONAL BOOKS

NEW YORK • TORONTO • LONDON • AUCKLAND • SYDNEY

Dedication

A special thanks to my husband, Harry, and my sons, Sean, Brian, and Colin, for their never-ending encouragement and support in my effort to guide children to love learning

and

to all of the children, parents, and educators whose lives I have touched who also embrace the idea that strong literacy is the root of achieving life's dreams.

Scholastic Inc. grants teachers permission to photocopy the activity sheets from this book for classroom use. No other part of this publication may be reproduced in whole or in part, or stored in a retrieval system, or transmitted in any form or by any means, electronic or mechanical, photocopying, recording, or otherwise, without written permission of the publisher.
For information regarding permission, write to Scholastic Inc., 730 Broadway, New York, NY 10003.

Designed by Jacqueline Swensen
Cover design by Vincent Ceci
Cover art by Donna Perone
Interior illustration by Maxie Chambliss
Photographs by Karen Grindall
ISBN 0-590-49353-1

Copyright © 1993 by Scholastic Inc. All rights reserved.

12 11 10 9 8 7 6 5 4 3 2 1   1 2 3 4 5/9

Printed in the U.S.A.

Table of Contents

Introduction	4

∾ SECTION ONE ∾
Assessing Your Own Literacy Beliefs — 5

Formulating Your Whole Language Philosophy and Goals	6
Self-Assessment Worksheet: Whole Language Philosophy	8
Self-Assessment Worksheet: Setting Professional Goals	10
Sample Statement of Philosophy and Goals	11
Worksheet: My Literacy Philosophy and Professional Goals	12

∾ SECTION TWO ∾
Literacy Empowerment: Children — 13

I Can/I Am Responsible	14
Thumbs Voting	15
Class Meetings	16
Teaching Students to Think	17
Word Rings	18
Author Notebook	21
Spin-Off Stories	22
Cross-Age Buddies	25
Good Guy Sign-In	26
Language Notebook	27
Table Names That Teach	28
Big Poetry	29
Poetry Kid for the Day	30
Time-Out Tape	31
Pattern Books	32
Cooperative Learning: Getting Young Children Going	34
Class Photo Journal	36
Homework Help	38
Walking Word Board	40
Take-Home Backpacks	41
Response Journal	45

∾ SECTION THREE ∾
Literacy Empowerment: Teachers — 47

Mini Literacy Diaries	48
Creating Materials Files	49
Find It Fast	50
A Ditto Alternative	51
Choosing and Using Literature	52
Resource Planning Book	53
Teachers Helping Teachers	54
Webbing a Lesson	56

∾ SECTION FOUR ∾
Literacy Empowerment: Parents and the Community — 59

Involving Parents	60
Weekly Letter to Parents	66
Parents As Reading Partners	67
Listening Volunteers	70
Tapping Community Resources	75
Parent Backpacks	76
Literacy Heroes	78
Open-Door Friends	80

Introduction

It's exciting to hear so many teachers talking about moving toward a more natural way of teaching—cradled in a basic whole language philosophy. Whole language is rooted in an understanding that language cannot be compartmentalized or segmented. It is an understanding that speaking, reading, writing, and listening need to be woven throughout a child's experiences. Whole language is *not* a collection of teaching methods. Instead, it's a philosophy about strengthening all aspects of a child's language development.

To be effective in implementing and developing such an approach, you need to build a strong foundation in whole language philosophy. A good place to begin is by talking with your colleagues. Share thoughts about literacy, information from readings, practical teaching ideas and strategies. Take time to do some professional reading. This doesn't have to mean reading a book cover to cover. Choose chapters that address your specific areas of interest.

To take your whole language program beyond a beginning stage, it is imperative that you use the information you gather to formulate your own whole language philosophy, not just clone one from someone else. The first section in this book is designed to help you use what you know and learn about yourself to develop your own philosophy and set of goals for using a whole language approach in your classroom. You'll find self-assessment sheets to guide you in putting your philosophy and goals into writing. The process is a little like designing a new piece of clothing. You have to first assess your needs, your desires, your materials, and your resources before you can proceed with a design. When you put the pieces together, you'll have a philosophy tailor-made for you, one that empowers you to guide children in their language development in the best way you can.

Section 2 continues with step-by-step descriptions of strategies and activities for moving your whole language program forward by helping children take responsibility for their learning. Section 3 contains tools for organizing, for asssessment and review, and for choosing and using literature. I hope this section will help you grow in your ability to create a strong, rich literacy environment for your students.

Finally, Section 4 deals with school-home/community communication—getting parents involved both in and out of the classroom and using the people in your community as additional classroom resources. Together, the four sections are designed to empower you, your students, parents, and the community to build a successful learning environment.

A small picture frame sits on my desk, encasing four lines of powerful words. I often reflect on the piece, especially when everything isn't as perfect as I want it to be:

> If you can imagine it,
> You can achieve it.
> If you can dream it,
> You can become it!

I hope this book helps you imagine, achieve, dream, and become the best literacy facilitator you can for your students. Remember, they will run our world when you and I sit in our rocking chairs. Give them strong roots to do a good job!

Karen Grindall

SECTION ONE

Assessing Your Own Literacy Beliefs

Formulating Your Whole Language Philosophy and Goals

∞ PURPOSE ∞

To make a philosophical change in your teaching, you first must take ownership of your own philosophy. Professional reading is an important part of formulating your philosophy, but you can't just read someone else's book and say "That's the philosophy I want to adopt." You must take time to carefully assess your strengths, your weaknesses, your perception of long-term goals for children in the learning process, your background knowledge, your dominant learning style, and so on. Remember that your students will learn best when they feel that you are secure in and excited about facilitating new knowledge.

You might be tempted to turn right to the other sections in this book for teaching strategies and ideas that you can use in your classroom. But please take the time to give yourself a base for your curriculum delivery before you do so. As you complete the self-assessment sheets on pages 8–10, characteristics of your philosophy will begin to emerge: how you feel about assessment, about scheduling, about student-teacher roles, and so on. You'll also begin to identify areas for improvement. Finally, you can use the form on page 12 to streamline and record your philosophy and goals. On page 11 you will find a statement of my current philosophy and goals. You can use this as a guide in formulating your own philosophy and in setting professional goals for your own growth.

∞ MATERIALS ∞

○ Self-Assessment Worksheet: Whole Language Philosophy (see reproducible on page 8)

○ Self-Assessment Worksheet: Setting Professional Goals (see reproducible on page 10)

○ Worksheet: My Literacy Philosophy and Professional Goals (see reproducible on page 12)

∞ HOW TO USE ∞

You will be working to construct statements in two categories:

○ your literacy philosophy

○ your professional growth goals for this school year

1. Make sure you have read articles and books on whole language. (Skim the table of contents for key sections that can help you strengthen your knowledge base.) Instead of focusing on one author, become familiar with a variety of viewpoints. Become a regular reader of periodicals

such as *Reading Teacher, Instructor,* and *Educational Leadership*. Check your local library, your school library, and your local teacher training institution for available materials. Always keep in mind that you are working on forming your own philosophy, not cloning one that belongs to another educator or author.

2. Once you have developed an awareness of the general philosophy of whole language, decide how much of a purist you feel you need to be. Because my class is made up of children with different learning styles, I find a multifaceted approach best meets their learning needs.

3. Use the worksheet on pages 8 and 9 to begin to assess yourself. This can be difficult to do, and you might want to spread the process over several days. I keep an assessment worksheet in an appointment notebook that I carry with me so that I can work on it when I have spare time.

4. Review the sheet and circle key words and statements that you feel strongly about. Think about why these words and statements mean so much to you as you begin to formulate statements about your philosophy. Use the form on page 12 to record these thoughts. Be realistic; three to five statements is usually sufficient.

5. Ask a mentor or close colleague to read your statements and to suggest revisions.

6. Using the assessment sheet on page 10, follow the same procedure to identify yearly goals. Consider one area of the curriculum that you, as a professional, need to focus on for growth. To strengthen your foundation in whole language, you might begin by setting goals in reading and writing. As you become stronger in your philosophy, you can learn more about weaving language into math and other content areas.

7. Prepare a final copy of page 12 that includes both your philosophy and your goals. Tape a copy to your desk, to the front of your plan book, or to some other visible place for a ready reminder. Finally, share a copy with parents at Back-to-School night or during parent-teacher conferences.

⁂ REFLECTIONS ⁂

So often when I present workshops, teachers want "recipes" to make whole language work for them in their classroom. I can give you many strategies, but if you declare that you have a "whole language classroom" and it is built solely on techniques rather than your working from your own philosophy base, then you are still trapped in a methods approach to teaching. It is important that you become clear about your philosophy and that you continue to set goals that will help you implement your philosophy to effectively change education for your children.

Self-Assessment Worksheet

∽ WHOLE LANGUAGE PHILOSOPHY ∽

This worksheet is a way to help you learn more about yourself as a teacher. As you work through it, look for and circle key words. These are the building blocks of your literacy philosophy and will help you pull all of your thoughts together in three to five capsule statements that present a clear picture of your literacy philosophy.

1. What is my role in the classroom?
   _____
   _____

2. What is the role of children in the classroom?
   _____
   _____

3. How do I feel about:
   noise _____
   parent involvement _____
   grouping _____
   tracking _____
   nontraditional assessment _____
   worksheets _____
   curriculum integration _____
   adhering to a daily schedule _____
   giving children responsible freedom in learning choices
   _____

4. Words that I often use to describe strong literacy are:
   _____

5. What are some needs of my students?
   _____
   _____

6. What am I best at giving to children to strengthen literacy?
   _____
   _____

7. What area of the curriculum am I most comfortable with?
   _____
   _____

8. What are my own learning styles?

9. Which professional authors do I most enjoy reading?

10. What key words or concepts from these authors am I most attracted to?

11. Am I more comfortable using strategies or methods in my teaching?

12. Do I consider myself a whole language purist? Or am I eclectic, a gatherer of many strategies?

13. Do I integrate literature into many areas of the curriculum, or do I prefer to use literature books for reading?

14. Do I need to be in charge, or am I comfortable being a facilitator?

15. Do I feel a need to stay with a planned schedule, or am I more comfortable adapting a lesson as children's needs arise?

16. What do I believe makes a student successful?

17. Am I comfortable using alternatives to worksheets and traditional assessment methods?

18. As a teacher, what philosophy or thinking background have I come from?

19. As a teacher, how do I interact with my students on a daily basis? Is there anything about this role that I would like to modify?

Self-Assessment Worksheet

⊗ SETTING PROFESSIONAL GOALS ⊗

I strongly recommend that you select at least one but no more than four professional growth goals for the school year. Setting too many goals may make it difficult for you to see and achieve real growth. Answering the following questions can help you target areas for growth.

1. What are my strongest curriculum areas? Why?

   _____
   _____
   _____
   _____
   _____

2. What area of the curriculum do I want to strengthen? Why?

   _____
   _____
   _____
   _____
   _____

3. Why is this area not as strong as I would like it to be?

   _____
   _____
   _____
   _____
   _____

4. How can I strengthen this area?

   _____ workshops

   _____ professional reading (books, periodicals)

   _____ college-level classes

   _____ training sessions

   _____ projects I design for classroom use

   _____ teacher networking

   _____ acquiring and using new materials

   _____ professional organizations

Sample Statement of Philosophy and Goals

ᴄᴏ MY WHOLE LANGUAGE ᴄᴏ PHILOSOPHY

To help my students become strong, literate, lifelong learners, I want to encourage them in these areas:

- **ownership**—To motivate children to feel that they are learning because they want to, not because they have to please others.

- **risk taking**—Each of us has a different level of risk-taking willingness. I will work hard to support children in their curiosity and risk taking so that they grow as self-starters in the learning process.

- **flexibility**—All children are not alike. I have a class of individual learners. It is important that I am flexible with their emotional and intellectual growth.

ᴄᴏ MY PROFESSIONAL ᴄᴏ GOALS FOR THIS YEAR

To continue to grow as a professional, I will focus on:

- strengthening my ability to integrate content areas more intensely into the reading-writing program, especially in science.

- improving my ability to use higher-order problem-solving techniques in stretching students' curiosity.

- further integrating telecommunications and other technology into the entire curriculum.

- deepening the classroom connections between the arts and the language curriculum.

Worksheet

MY LITERACY PHILOSOPHY AND PROFESSIONAL GOALS

LITERACY PHILOSOPHY

To help children become strong, lifelong, literate learners, I will guide them in these areas:

○ _____

○ _____

○ _____

○ _____

PROFESSIONAL GOALS FOR THIS YEAR

To continue to grow as a professional, I will focus on these areas:

○ _____

○ _____

○ _____

○ _____

SECTION TWO

Literacy Empowerment: Children

I Can/I Am Responsible

◯∽ PURPOSE ∽◯

Just as you set goals for your own growth, it's important to help children set goals for themselves. Starting from the first day of school, I stress two phrases: *I Can* and *I Am Responsible*. I recognize students' strengths and areas of need, but at the same time I want them to believe that they can do their very best. These two phrases help transfer ownership of this goal to the children.

∽ MATERIALS ∽

- Signs with the words *I Can* and *I Am Responsible*

∽ HOW TO USE ∽

1. Initiate a discussion about what *I can* means by reading *The Little Engine That Could* by Watty Piper (Putnam Publishing Group). Invite children to share their interpretaions of the phrase. Encourage them to tell about times they felt like the little engine.

2. Follow up with a discussion of the statement *I am responsible*. Present children with "what if" situations such as the following: You are walking down the steps and push the child in front of you to get ahead. Ask children to describe what might happen as a result of this action. Help them recognize that each person is responsible for choosing the best way to behave.

3. Ask children to help you post signs that say *I can* and *I am responsible* in several places around the room.

4. Reinforce both phrases often, especially in incidental learning situations. For example, when you're reading aloud, ask students to point out characters whose behavior or actions represent either phrase.

∽ REFLECTIONS ∽

Perhaps one of the biggest mistakes we make in our classrooms is that we let ourselves be the person who corrects, the person who lets students know what is right and wrong. Transferring this judgment to students is important: there won't always be a teacher or parent to make those decisions for them. Encouraging students to evaluate their own behaviors and actions also helps them become safe risk takers.

Thumbs Voting

∽ PURPOSE ∾

It's so easy to ask a question and let children respond by raising their hands and waiting to be called on. But what about students who are hesitant risk takers and will not raise a hand unless they feel "safe" with their answers? Or children who are impulsive and raise their hands without first carefully considering their answers? Here's a technique that gives every child a chance to think of the best answer and to respond. And it gives you an opportunity to learn more about all of your students' thinking processes.

∽ HOW TO USE ∾

1. In this exercise, children use their hands to indicate answers. There are three ways to indicate an answer: thumbs up (to indicate yes), thumbs down (to indicate no), or hands flat out (to indicate maybe).

2. Begin by posing a question. For example, part way through reading *The Giving Tree* by Shel Silverstein (HarperCollins Children's Books), ask: "Do you think the tree is really happy?" Students respond with thumbs up, thumbs down, or hands flat. Encourage children to choose their own responses rather than look at how others are responding.

3. You might follow up by asking children to explain their answers.

∽ REFLECTIONS ∾

This technique is effective with yes and no questions as well as with questions that require students to make predictions. Though it is not intended to serve as an individual assessment tool, it is an effective group assessment tool and can give you immediate feedback about general understanding.

∽ EXTENSIONS ∾

○ Math: Use, for example, with story problems to show whether students need to add or subtract

○ Language arts: Use, for example, to show whether a plural is formed by adding -*s* (thumbs up) or -*es* (thumbs down) to a word, or to find out if students would change the ending of a story (follow with discussion).

Class Meetings

∽ PURPOSE ∽

A sense of community not only makes the classroom a safer, more secure place to be, it also enables cooperative learning to take place. But sometimes students need some help building bonds. Several years ago I had a group of children who had a difficult time accepting each other. I implemented a process I call class meetings to help all of us look at the positive parts of each other's personalities and to begin to work together more positively as a group.

∽ HOW TO USE ∽

1. Gather children together in a large open area in the classroom.

2. Establish basic ground rules, including:

- the circle must be inclusive: no one may sit outside or inside.
- you may not talk when another child is talking.
- as discussion proceeds around the circle, you have the right to respond or pass. (I tell students they will not be allowed to pass every time.)
- after we go around the circle, then you may make additional comments (but not negative statements or put-downs about classmates' comments).

3. Select a nonthreatening topic for each class meeting. Open-ended sentences are particularly effective because they give all children a place to start and let them use their own creativity, feelings, and ideas to complete the thoughts. For example, you might ask students to complete a sentence such as "My favorite story is...." Other starters include the following:

- I am really good at...
- A good friend is someone who...
- I wish adults would...
- If I could go to a faraway place, I would go to... because...
- The hardest thing for me to do is...
- I feel sad when...
- I hope the president will...

∽ REFLECTIONS ∽

Class meetings help get children in the habit of interacting in positive ways and contribute to an overall positive atmosphere in the classroom. (I never hold class meetings to deal with problems because then the activity becomes a "trial by jury.") This activity is also an effective way to let children respond to literature. For example, you might give them an incomplete sentence such as: "My favorite person in the story is... because...."

Teaching Students to Think

✦ PURPOSE ✦

Teaching students to stop and identify problems and to work through a thinking process before reaching conclusions is as relevant to learning as core curriculum. Techniques such as the five-step process described here can be integrated into all subject areas.

✦ MATERIALS ✦

○ a poster-size display of the following five steps:

1. Tell us about the problem.

2. Make a list of all the ways someone could handle this problem.

3. Go back and carefully read all the ways again.

4. Pick the best way to handle the problem.

5. Think about this choice one more time before you act.

✦ HOW TO USE ✦

1. Brainstorm the kinds of decisions students make every day. If necessary, start them off with an example such as the following: A friend always takes your markers without asking. What would you do? Talk about the way children normally decide on what to do.

2. Use the poster to introduce the five-step process for problem solving. Post the chart in a visible place.

3. In a large group session, pose some problems, being careful not to choose any that will result in particular children being singled out.

4. Invite a child to volunteer another problem. Let the class use the five-step process to come up with possible solutions. Stress the importance of steps 3 and 5.

5. Once the thinking-process pattern is established, use it with students to solve class problems.

✦ REFLECTIONS ✦

I find that children react to this five-step process very positively, almost with relief that there is a process to help them make better decisions. Once students become accustomed to thinking about the decisions they make, you will most likely see growth in their abilities to work with cause and effect, predictions, and other higher levels of thinking.

✦ EXTENSIONS ✦

Give students opportunities to practice using the five-step process with situations from literature. For example, have them help Alexander in *Alexander and the Terrible, Horrible, No Good, Very Bad Day* by Judith Viorst (Macmillan Children's Book Group) as one difficulty after another arises. This exercise not only helps students understand story characters better but also provides modeling situations for students' daily decision making.

Word Rings

◌ PURPOSE ◌

Word cards or flash cards are a way of building children's rote knowledge base. But often the cards are used a few times to drill and are then put away. Instead, put a set of cards into each of your students' hands. In this way they'll have a chance to see the words again and again, as many times as they need or want to. For visual learners, this is especially important.

◌ MATERIALS ◌

- metal shower curtain rings
- 20" length of ribbon for each child (optional)
- word card form (see reproducible on page 20)
- duplicating paper or heavy stock paper that can go through the copy machine
- laminating film (not absolutely necessary but strongly recommended to improve durability)
- hole punch

◌ HOW TO MAKE ◌

1. Make copies of the word card form.

2. List selected words in the first column, one per rectangle. Repeat the same words in the remaining two horizontal columns. This is your master word sheet.

3. Make enough copies of the master word sheet so that each child gets one vertical word strip or column. (The form is set up to create word strips for three students per page.)

4. Laminate the sheet for durability, and then cut the columns apart.

5. Punch a hole on the left-hand side of

every rectangle to enable children to put individual cards on the shower rings.

⌘ HOW TO USE ⌘

1. After working with a new big book or other story, choose words to focus on for structure and vocabulary. Write these words on the master word sheet. (I also write these words on 3" x 5" index cards for use in group work.) There are 10 spaces available in each column. You may want to leave a couple blank so that children can add their own words.

2. Before children cut the word strips apart, check their ability to say the words in isolation (after using them many times in context). If they say a word correctly, punch a hole on the right side of that rectangle. Children then cut the word strips apart and put the cards on their rings.

Activities to try before students put their word cards on the rings include the following:

- sorting words by blends, by initial letters, by ending letters, and so on
- putting the cards in alphabetical order
- choosing a word and using it in a question or statement
- making words plural
- adding endings to the words
- finding a sentence in the story with the word in it and reading the sentence
- giving a synonym or antonym for a word

⌘ REFLECTIONS ⌘

When I conference with a child's parent, I always use the word ring as another way of discussing assessment. It gives a fairly clear picture of a child's capabilities in identifying specific words in isolation. My first graders sometimes wear their word rings on a length of ribbon. When we stand in line for the restroom, they practice the words with a classmate. Some days I bring the hole punch along. As students recognize more words without help, I punch the right side of their cards.

I often take four or five minutes of class time and have the children go through the words, first alone and then with a friend. This way, even though we have finished a book, children have constant exposure to the vocabulary and can master the words with repetition. The next time a child picks up that story, he or she will have the excitement of knowing more words.

⌘ EXTENSIONS ⌘

Other ways you can use this same technique:
- math facts
- state names
- foreign language words
- spelling words
- months of the year
- geography terms
- planets

∽ WORD RINGS REPRODUCIBLE ∽

Author Notebook

✥ PURPOSE ✥

As we expose children to good literature and encourage them to write, we also need to provide good role models to help them believe that they too are worthy writers. One way to provide these role models is to familiarize students with authors of children's literature. Publications that feature articles about children's authors (and often include photographs) are a handy resource. And an author notebook is an easy way to organize the information so that you can quickly find an author whose book you are reading. An easy-to-make display board facilitates sharing the information with children.

✥ MATERIALS ✥

- author information and pictures of authors
- 8½" x 11" heavy stock paper
- paste
- laminating film
- three-ring binder
- notebook divider tabs
- large foam core board (check art or office supply stores)
- plastic clips with adhesive backs (check office supply stores)

✥ HOW TO USE ✥

1. Collect pictures and information about different authors from sources such as:

- children's book club catalogues
- professional magazines (such as *Instructor*'s Meet the Author and Poetry Pages)
- books about authors, such as *Bill Peet: An Autobiography* by Bill Peet (Houghton Mifflin)
- author resources from your public library, such as reference books and biographies

2. Try to include pictures, personal information, the author's thoughts about writing, a book jacket if possible, and a mailing address if available.

3. Cut, trim, and mount the pictures and information on heavy stock paper. Laminate each page.

4. Place pages in the binder with a divider tab in front of each author section.

5. Prepare a display board by scoring the foam core board so that it creases and stands up. Make a title for the board such as Come Meet a New Author. Attach plastic clips so that you can easily display pages about a particular author.

6. When you focus on a new book or author, remove the appropriate pages from the binder and clip them to the board.

✥ REFLECTIONS ✥

I like to use the foam core display board instead of a bulletin board because it's easy to bring to the large group area. I've also found that children are more responsive to the display board than to a bulletin board. They enjoy moving it to a table top and reading it together. I used to create a display board for each author, but this method created serious storage problems. By keeping one notebook, you and your students can readily locate information on particular authors. And the single display board is easily stored.

Spin-Off Stories

⸺ PURPOSE ⸺

One way to help children learn that there are different points of view to any one action is to create spin-off stories from literature. By changing at least one of the story elements—characters, setting, or plot—and retelling a story, children become more aware of different points of view. With practice, they'll become better able to apply this understanding to their everyday lives.

⸺ MATERIALS ⸺

- a favorite story
- chart paper
- marker
- 12" x 18" construction paper
- drawing supplies
- computer or typewriter

⸺ HOW TO MAKE ⸺

1. Read a good, simple book that lends itself to a spin-off. (Not all good books work well as spin-offs. See page 24 for story suggestions.)

2. Ask children how they could change the character, setting, or plot yet retain the story's pattern.

3. On chart paper, create a story structure sheet to use as a framework to map out the story from another point of view. Let students take turns telling what happens next. Record students' sentences on the chart paper, leaving spaces between lines. This way, if students decide that they've skipped something, you can include the sentence in the proper sequence. Let students refer to the original book as often as necessary so that they can maintain the basic story structure.

4. When students are satisfied with the story, number each sentence, then cut the sentences apart. Depending on the number of sentences, let individuals or pairs of children select sentences to illustrate.

5. Have children illustrate their sentences on 12" x 18" construction paper, leaving a space for the sentences at the top. (My students leave a space that measures four fingers wide.)

6. Type sentences on a computer or typewriter, using large-size print. Paste them on the corresponding illustrations.

7. Have a child design a cover illustration, then laminate and bind the pages to make a book.

HOW TO USE

Spin-off stories become a treasured part of the classroom library. They have other uses as well, including the following:

- as a big book for students to share with other classes
- as a book to take home and read to a parent (I made some take-home bags out of scrap denim fabric to protect books going to and from home.)
- as a model for children to create their own spin-off stories

REFLECTIONS

I want to encourage children to take risks in their learning. But many of us are hesitant illustrators. Though I want to encourage children to take risks in their illustrations, they can't do this if they're worried about "ruining" final book pages. That's why I do the sentence printing separately from the illustrations. We talk in our large group circle about how everything doesn't always come out the way we want but that mistakes are okay as long as we are working seriously.

EXTENSIONS

Take a closer look at such spin-off stories as Raymond Briggs's *Jim and the Beanstalk* (Putnam Publishing Group) and Jon Scieszka's *The True Story of the Three Little Pigs* (Viking Children's Books). Students also enjoy writing spin-offs of children's songs, especially those by Bill Harley. My class enjoys his cassette "Come Out and Play" (Round River Records).

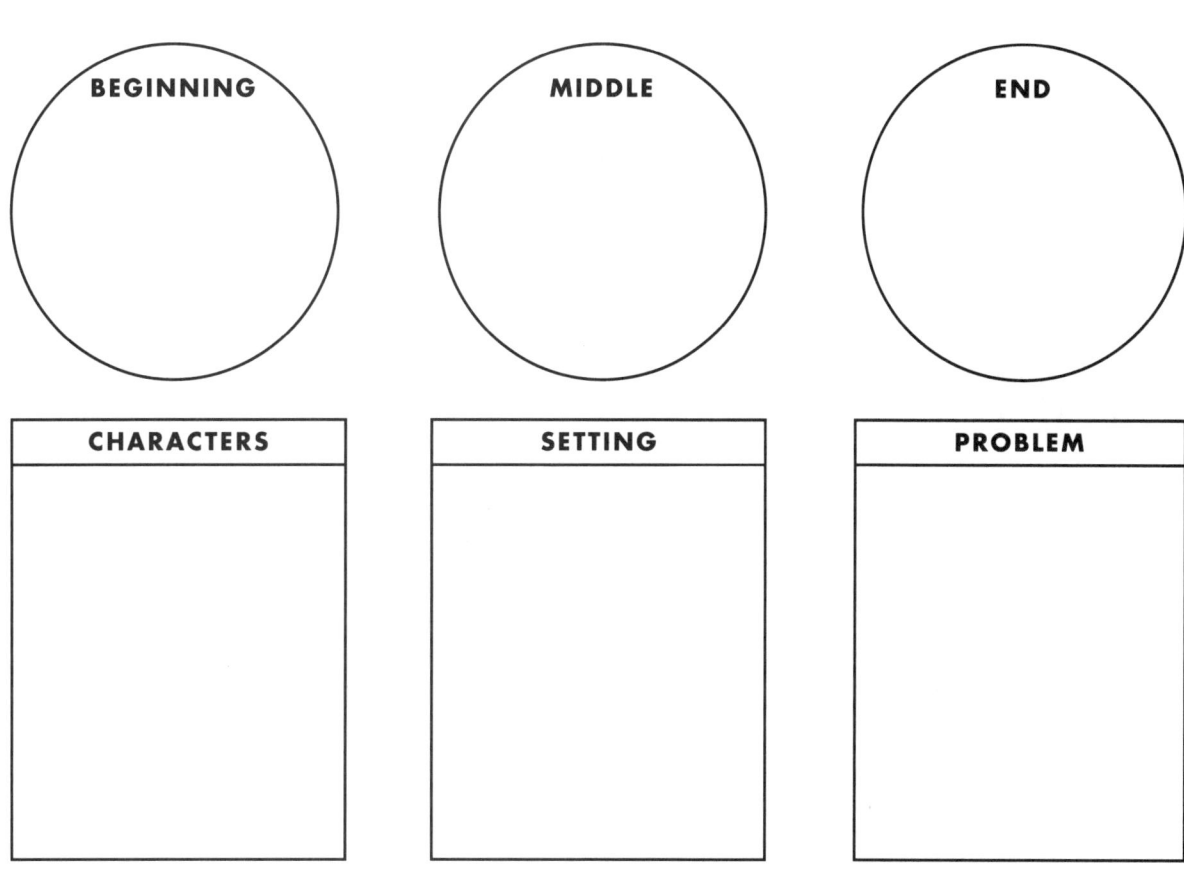

FOR A STORY STRUCTURE SHEET

BEGINNING / MIDDLE / END

CHARACTERS / SETTING / PROBLEM

Favorite Books for Spin-off Stories

Goodnight Moon
by Margaret Wise Brown
(HarperCollins Children's Books)
- spin-off suggestion: Good Morning Sun

Runaway Bunny
by Margaret Wise Brown
(HarperCollins Children's Books)
- spin-off suggestion: Runaway Kitty

A Chair for My Mother
by Vera B. Williams
(Morrow)
- spin-off suggestions: A Car for My Father or A Hat for My Grandmother

The Very Hungry Caterpillar
by Eric Carle
(Putnam Publishing Group)
- spin-off suggestion: The Very Hungry First Grader

Freight Train
by Donald Crews
(Morrow)
- spin-off suggestion: any other vehicle

Are You My Mother?
by Phillip D. Eastman
(Random House Books for Young Readers)
- spin-off suggestion: any other family member or pet

Harold and the Purple Crayon
by Crockett Johnson
(HarperCollins Children's Books)
- spin-off suggestion: change to chalk or paint

The Snowy Day
by Ezra Jack Keats
(Puffin Books)
- spin-off suggestions: The Rainy Day or The Windy Day

Listen to the Rain
by Bill Martin Jr. & John Archambault
(Henry Holt & Co.)
- spin-off suggestion: Listen to the Wind

Alexander and the Terrible, Horrible, No Good, Very Bad Day
by Judith Viorst
(Macmillan Children's Book Group)
- spin-off suggestion: change to a good day or remake the character

Quick As a Cricket
by Don Wood
(Child's Play)
- spin-off suggestion: make a whole new book of similes

There are many other great books for inspiring spin-off stories. Just remember that the story line must be simple enough for children to follow the pattern.

Cross-Age Buddies

∽ PURPOSE ∽

Cross-age buddy programs give students special learning opportunities. Younger children benefit from having a friend to read with, someone who can give extra one-on-one attention, and a role model that they may not have in an older sibling. The buddy program also benefits older children who gain practice applying concepts in ways that younger children can understand.

∽ HOW TO USE ∽

1. Team up with an upper-grade teacher who wants to participate in a cross-age buddy program.

2. Together, sit down with both class lists and discuss children's personalities, needs, interests, and so on. Try to match children so that they complement each other, but keep in mind that you can make adjustments later if necessary.

3. Identify goals, activities you would like to implement, and time periods when children will get together. It's important that this time is viewed as a collaborative learning project, not just a time to visit.

4. To avoid miscommunication that could jeopardize the success of the program, make sure that you put all of the above decisions in writing and that each of you has a copy.

5. Make sure that the older children in this project understand that they are role models for the younger children but not their bosses. Encourage class discussion on ways they can be good role models.

6. Spend the first few sessions on activities designed to help students get to know each other. For example, have buddies interview each other or read a favorite story together.

∽ REFLECTIONS ∽

As students get to know each other, they often start writing notes back and forth. We are fortunate to have our computers linked so that students can type messages in our room that their buddies can print out in their room. Some of our favorite activities combine play with curriculum. For example, a science lesson on surface tension culminated on the playground with a bubble-making experiment.

Good Guy Sign-In

◯ PURPOSE ◯

To strengthen positive behavior in the classroom, I try to make examples of appropriate behavior more frequently than I correct negative behavior.

◯ MATERIALS ◯

- 12" x 18" pieces of paper to use as Good Guy Sign-In sheets (include date and team names)
- library book pocket or envelope
- stickers

◯ HOW TO USE ◯

1. Create teams based on the class seating arrangement. For example, in my classroom, student desks are grouped into two long tables, forming two teams.

2. Give each team a name (see page 28 for suggestions on choosing table names).

3. Write the name of each team on a 12" x 18" sheet of paper. Post the sheets on a chalkboard or bulletin board.

4. Place stickers in the library book pocket and post near the team sheets.

5. Whenever a child is displaying good behavior, have the child sign his or her team sheet.

6. Whenever an entire team is modeling good behavior, such as getting ready quietly for a class meeting, place a sticker on that team's sheet.

7. At the end of the week, reward the team with the most signatures and stickers with a treat such as new pencils, stickers, or a special privilege.

8. Start with a fresh sheet for each team the following week.

◯ REFLECTIONS ◯

So often we start a school year off with the intention that we will focus on good behavior. Yet, as the year progresses, we find ourselves spending more time on corrective comments. I find the good guy sheet not only helps children choose correct behavior, but it also reminds me to praise students for that behavior. This simple activity also builds a sense of teamwork in a positive way.

For a variation, try focusing on a particular behavior one week, such as listening skills or homework completion.

Language Notebook

⊗ PURPOSE ⊗

Rather than use a traditional language arts textbook, I have children create their own resource books in which to collect materials related to their language development. These books belong to the children and therefore encourage them to assume ownership of their language development. Some items are the same for the entire class while others vary from child to child.

⊗ MATERIALS ⊗

- three-ring binder for each student
- a single sheet of heavy stock paper for each student to make a cover page
- laminating film (optional)
- a name sticker for the cover of each binder
- a set of tab dividers for each student

⊗ HOW TO USE ⊗

1. Give each child a piece of heavy stock paper on which to design a title page. Laminate it if possible. Have children put their title pages at the front of their binders.

2. Give each child a name sticker to identify his or her notebook.

3. Add the first section together. For example, have students copy their high-frequency word list, make a tab for this section, and add both the list and the tab to their notebooks.

4. Have children add other sections of their choosing, such as an ongoing, personal list of new words to use in stories, a mini-lesson on using quotations in story writing, an "About Me" inventory (see reproducible on page 65), a learning styles survey to help children identify the ways they learn best, favorite poems, story analysis sheets, and so on. Refer to students' books often to encourage a sense of value and usefulness.

5. Stress organization. It's not as important that the books be thick as it is that they are well-organized reference tools.

⊗ REFLECTIONS ⊗

These notebooks give children an opportunity to take ownership of their language development and of their growth in learning. The books become one of the many resources children can use to acquire and apply new information. As children add to and use their books, they begin to understand that knowledge isn't something that is simply stored in their heads. The notebooks help children organize information for future retrieval, strengthen study skills, and provide a sense of ongoing learning.

Table Names That Teach

◌ PURPOSE ◌

Giving names to groups of students can facilitate lining up and calling children together for small or large group activities. Instead of going for cute names, why not make these names work? By choosing names that relate to curriculum areas, you can promote and reinforce concepts you're covering in class.

◌ MATERIALS ◌

○ heavy paper or cardboard for name tags
○ bulldog clips

◌ HOW TO USE ◌

1. At the beginning of the year make a list of key concept words that you need to make sure your children know. Instead of calling a table of children by names such as Bears and Lions, for example, you might name one table Atlantic Ocean and the other Pacific Ocean.

2. Once children are familiar with the names, spend some large group instruction time learning more about them. You might take time each day to let students locate the Atlantic and Pacific oceans on a map. Reinforce the connection between the word and what it represents often during the weeks that you use these names.

3. When students are more familiar with their name and its concept, have them work together to design a giant name tag for their group. Encourage them to add illustrations or words that tell something about their name. To display, hang string from the ceiling and attach the tags with bulldog clips.

4. Later in the year you may want to change table names approximately once a month.

◌ REFLECTIONS ◌

This technique is especially effective with concepts that may otherwise be somewhat difficult for students to grasp. As you call groups together for different reasons throughout the day, the repetition enables children to more quickly learn the unfamiliar terms. Other key concept words you might want to use include the following:

○ names of continents
○ major United States cities
○ land formations
○ parts of speech
○ names of countries
○ science terms

Big Poetry

∽ PURPOSE ∾

One of the most basic concepts in the whole language philosophy is the understanding that language is filled with rhyme, rhythm, and repetition and that these 3Rs need to be part of children's literature experiences. Poetry has natural ingredients of rhyme, rhythm, and repetition and should be shared with children at all grade levels, not just with beginning readers. Daily shared reading of poetry strengthens children's use of language by exposing them to many rich, descriptive words that express ideas. A big book approach can facilitate sharing poetry with your students and, at the same time, help you meet the needs of both auditory and visual learners.

∽ MATERIALS ∾

- a selection of poems
- a copy machine for enlarging print
- 12" x 18" copy paper
- 12" x 18" heavy stock paper or construction paper
- laminating film

∽ HOW TO MAKE ∾

1. Choose poems with lots of rhyme, rhythm, or repetition, preferably on topics you are learning about.

2. Make enlarged photocopies of the poems, using big-book-size print.

3. Trim and mount poems on heavy stock paper or construction paper and laminate.

∽ REFLECTIONS ∾

I always mount poems on the same size paper so that they can be easily stored. I use these big-book-size poems much the same as I do big books—for large group language activities. We talk about what certain words mean, find adjectives, look for words that rhyme or begin with blends, locate words that express action, and so on. After we work with poems together, I make the pages available for students to use during their free choice time.

Poetry Kid for the Day

∽ PURPOSE ∽

Children benefit from having poetry read to them. In addition, by having children learn to select poetry to share with others, you give them opportunities to explore topics and styles that you may not necessarily choose. This activity helps transfer the selection process to children by designating special days and ways for children to share their poetry choices.

∽ MATERIALS ∽

- school year calendar
- simple cardboard badge saying Poetry Kid
- bell
- lots of poetry books
- empty binder for creating an *Our Favorite Poetry* anthology

∽ HOW TO USE ∽

1. Post a calendar and invite children to sign up to share some of their poetry selections. You might want to limit the activity to two or three days per month so that it does not lose its special glamour.

2. Have students select one or two poems they want to share with classmates and copy them on notebook paper.

3. On students' selected days, they get two items:

- a Poetry Kid badge
- a bell

At any time during the day (except, for example, when you're giving directions for an assignment), the Poetry Kid may ring the bell, signaling everyone to stop and listen to a poem.

4. Have students add the poems they read to the class poetry anthology. Keep the binder in the reading area so that students can read the poetry selections on their own or copy favorite poems into their notebooks or journals.

∽ REFLECTIONS ∽

As students begin to write their own poetry, I invite them to share their work and to add their poems to our poetry notebook. You can easily adapt the Poetry Kid approach to other areas. For example, if you are reading one of the witty and wacky *Amelia Bedelia* books by Peggy Parrish (HarperCollins Children's Books), invite students to share a riddle of the day, then write the riddle in a class riddle book. Or share story problems in math, or have students research and present amazing facts for a Did You Know? science book.

Time-Out Tape

⌘ PURPOSE ⌘

Children aren't always at their best for every lesson and can distract others around them. It's sometimes necessary to provide time out to allow students to refocus their attention. To provide for this without having students miss out on instruction or shared learning, I created a space we call time-out tape.

⌘ MATERIALS ⌘

○ a 10" piece of durable tape such as duct tape

⌘ HOW TO USE ⌘

1. Place the tape on the floor close to your large group instruction area.

2. When a child has difficulty attending during an activity or lesson, quietly tell the child to stand on the tape, or use body language to convey the message.

3. Let the student know when it is time to rejoin the group.

⌘ REFLECTIONS ⌘

We all have days when we have difficulty attending to a task. Sometimes it's more effective to remove children from situations they are not handling well rather than to continue reprimanding, reminding, or correcting. I like to involve students in deciding when they are ready to return to the group. In the beginning of the year, I might let students know when they can return. But later in the year, I let students decide when they are ready to rejoin the group. This technique lets learning continue with fewer interruptions and encourages students to take a stronger role in monitoring their own behavior.

Pattern Books

༄ PURPOSE ༄

When children begin to talk, we encourage them by promoting repetition. Teachers frequently use repetitive stories with beginning readers to help them get a feel for language. That's where repetition usually stops. But there are good reasons for using repetition as a teaching tool with emergent readers. Hearing a phrase or sentence repeated throughout a story helps children gain confidence in their reading ability, encouraging them to become successful lifelong readers.

One way to expose children to repetition is to create class pattern books. Begin by giving children a sentence starter; they supply words to complete the idea. By linking the theme of the pattern books to topics you're studying or to books you're reading, this activity helps support your curriculum at the same time. For example, if you're reading *The Snowy Day* by Ezra Jack Keats (Puffin Books), you can give children a chance to personalize the story by creating a pattern book that repeats the phrase "On a snowy day I like to_____."

༄ MATERIALS ༄

○ a page for each child with the same sentence starter written on each one. For example: "On my way to school I see _____." (See page 33 for more ideas for sentence starters.)

○ drawing materials

○ a visually appealing cover with the book title and a "copyright" page on the inside of the cover

○ laminating film

○ binding material

༄ HOW TO MAKE ༄

1. Give each child a copy of the sentence starter page. Do some brainstorming about the topic, and then have children write or dictate the rest of the sentence.

2. Have children illustrate their pages.

3. Decide on a title for the book and create a cover.

4. Laminate pages and bind them to make a book.

༄ REFLECTIONS ༄

I use pattern books to help children understand sentence structure and to reinforce certain skills. For example, we might do a pattern book using sentence starters that include possessives. Pattern books also encourage children to appreciate how their classmates think. I often contribute a page so that children can read about my ideas too.

Ideas for Sentence Starters

1. I feel scared when_____.

2. I love_____.

3. I'm (<u>cold</u>). Yes, I am (<u>cold</u>). (working with contractions)

4. This is (<u>Kate's mitten</u>). Isn't (<u>Kate's mitten</u>) (<u>warm</u>) ? (working with possessives)

5. I can help save the Earth when I_____.

6. I feel good when_____.

7. When I grow up I want to be a _____.

8. My hands can help me. My hands can close. My hands can open. My hands can _____. What can your hands do?

9. When (child's name) is (age), this is what he or she will look like!

10. On Saturday I like to_____.

11. This is a circle (a page with a circle on it). This was a circle but now it is a _____. (Children take the circle and make it into another object that has a circle shape in it, such as a donut. This activity can be done with any shape.)

12. (Make a list of direction words such as *up*, *down*, *out*, *in*, and so on. Have children use the words to complete the sentence.) (Child's name) went (direction word) the (place). For example: <u>Sam</u> went <u>down</u> the <u>street</u>.

13. I know a funny sound. It is (give a sound such as *plop*). A (something that makes that sound) goes (repeat the sound) when _____. For example: I know a funny sound. It is <u>plop</u>. A <u>raindrop</u> goes <u>plop</u> when <u>it hits a puddle</u>.

14. I can (write something child can do well). That's what I can do, can you?

Cooperative Learning: Getting Young Children Going

∽ PURPOSE ∽

Although many articles and books discuss cooperative learning, the activities are often directed at upper grades, where children have fairly strong abilities to record thoughts and observations in writing. In most first- and second-grade classrooms, the lack of writing ability could be a barrier. Consequently, many primary grade teachers shy away from cooperative learning in their classrooms. But this is really the time to lay the groundwork for this teaching tool. Then, as students become more proficient at expressing their ideas in writing, you can move smoothly into cooperative learning activities, even those that require recording ideas in writing.

∽ HOW TO USE ∽

1. Begin by holding class meetings. Simply gather children together in a circle on the floor, making sure that the circle is complete (no children are sitting farther in or out of the circle). Children should be able to see each other's faces. Let children know that this is a safe place for sharing thoughts and ideas.

2. Start with nonthreatening, open-ended sentences such as "My favorite food is_____because_____." I attempt to coax any shy children without too much pressure. After several weeks I then introduce the rule that students may choose not to answer only one time during

the week. Remember, very low-risk-taking children will take longer to volunteer than children who are more willing risk takers.

3. After about a month of nonthreatening topics, gradually introduce feeling statements such as

"I feel scared when_____" or

" I feel happy when_____."

4. As children begin to build more trust in vocalizing, move to more difficult discussions, again focusing on such nonthreatening topics as "What could I do if a friend started to bully me?" The success of this exercise is based on your ability to draw children into the discussion, not to become the giver of what you think they should believe.

5. As children become more open and trusting with each other, begin work on a cooperative activity for teams of two. Involve children in selecting partners by asking them to list (or tell you privately) the names of four classmates they think they would enjoy doing an art project with. If you can't meet every student's choice, talk with the class and explain that students will need to make some readjustments. It is important at this point to spend the time and effort getting good partner combinations so that fewer problems arise as children begin to work together.

6. In selecting a project or problem, keep in mind that students will be building partner trust. For this reason, it's wise to choose a nonthreatening activity that won't create a competitive relationship.

7. It is very important that you be a good "kid watcher" in this first cooperative learning experience. Conference with students who have trouble working together, focusing on their strengths, not weaknesses. Have them give four good suggestions about ways they might be able to solve their conflicts. If that technique does not work, let them know that their classmates might be able to give them suggestions. Invite them to present their problem at the next class meeting.

∽ REFLECTIONS ∽

Despite their name, cooperative learning activities can have their problems. Remember, you are uniting two or more children who have different backgrounds and personalities. The purpose of using cooperative learning in the classroom is to help children learn how to use their strengths and to draw on the strengths of fellow classmates for growth. Some days will be terrific. Other days, personality conflicts may cause you great concern. However, a good teacher is a good "kid watcher" and will continually observe children and try new ways to facilitate the learning process.

There are no special recipes to make cooperative learning work. But clear directions, strong classroom management, and a good sense of class community are important keys to its success. Allow several months to build a cooperative effort before moving students into cooperative learning activities. It is a growing process, not just an activity to do tomorrow.

Class Photo Journal

❧ PURPOSE ❧

Because many parents work during the school day and are unavailable to volunteer in the classroom, it's important to find other ways of keeping them connected with what's going on. A class photo journal is an excellent tool for keeping parents up to date on class activities and events, even daily routines. The journal is also a way of encouraging children's language development as they share the photos with their families.

❧ MATERIALS ❧

- camera and film
- computer or typewriter
- heavy stock paper
- laminating film
- hole punch
- three-ring binder
- Parent Comments page (see reproducible on page 37)

❧ HOW TO USE ❧

1. Keep an inexpensive, loaded camera in the classroom. You will probably find it easier to keep the album current if you use film with 12 exposures, thus processing film more frequently than with 24 or 36 exposures.

2. Photograph special activities as well as everyday happenings.

3. After processing, have children create two- to four-sentence captions that explain each photo.

4. Paste photos and typed explanations on heavy stock paper. Laminate pages, hole-punch, and add them to the notebook.

5. Add a title page, a brief explanation of the purpose of the book, and copies of the parent comments page.

❧ REFLECTIONS ❧

Photo journals are particularly helpful for children who aren't very vocal and may not offer much information when asked "What did you do in school today?" Instead, parents and children can use the photos as springboards for discussion. Because pages are added constantly, each child can take the book home to share new photos about every month and a half. My students really enjoy taking this book home to share. Parent response is also extremely positive.

❧ EXTENSIONS ❧

- Take pictures at the beginning of the school year and make duplicate prints. Display children's photos next to their stories, artwork, poetry, or other work.
- Take pictures of children engaged in positive or helpful activities. Add these photos to the journal to encourage discussion about behavior.
- Use a video camera to capture events from the school year. Make a copy for students to borrow and share with their families.

Class Photo Journal

∽ **PARENT COMMENTS** ∽

After looking at and discussing the photo journal with your child, please take a few minutes to complete this form. Make sure your child returns the journal to school tomorrow so that another child can take it home.

Child's name_____ Date_____

What was your child's favorite picture? Why?

_____

_____

What was your favorite picture? Why?

_____

_____

_____

What did you learn about your child's work at school from these pictures?

_____

_____

_____

_____

Additional parent and/or child comments:

_____

_____

_____

_____

Homework Help

❧ PURPOSE ❧

Choosing homework activities for children is as important as choosing classroom activities. Homework is most meaningful when it not only extends classroom curriculum but also deepens learning and arouses thinking. Homework that consists of ditto sheets filled with repetitive problems generally fails to stimulate thinking and learning. It also results in piles of papers to correct and presents management problems when children do not bring a completed assignment to class.

Here's a technique to help you manage homework, and delegate some responsibility to others appropriately.

❧ MATERIALS ❧

- weekly letter to parents that lists the week's homework (see page 66)
- check-off list of students' names (see reproducible on page 39)
- two-pocketed folder

❧ HOW TO USE ❧

1. Place copies of the check-off list in the left-hand pocket of the folder. Completed homework is placed in the right pocket.

2. Each week, select a different child to be homework checker. This child is responsible for collecting assignments, checking off students' names on the list, and placing the papers in the right-hand pocket of the folder. (To help younger children make sure they using the correct column of the check-off list, I run a highlighter over the column for the day.)

3. Ask children who turn homework in late to place it in the left-hand pocket so that you can check it off.

4. At the end of the week, I staple a copy of that week's parent letter to the check-off sheet and place it in a folder. Information on specific homework assignments is then readily available for parent conferences.

❧ REFLECTIONS ❧

Part of becoming a facilitator is learning to give responsibility to students and to involve them in the smooth, day-to-day running of their classroom. Using this homework management technique helps my students understand that they are part of the classroom process and reinforces their responsibility to complete and return homework.

It's also important to me to involve parents in their child's homework. Every Monday I send a letter to parents explaining what is going on in our class this week. At the end of this letter, I list homework assignments for the week. I choose assignments that correlate to the curriculum generally and not to a specific day's lesson. I am also cautious not to repeat the same type of activity in the week. For example, one night I might assign a problem-solving activity and another night ask children to read to their parents. (I make an effort to have one night's homework involve one or more additional family members.) Parents come to expect this letter and, with it, information about homework. The letter encourages parents to take an interest in their children's homework and helps them plan time to work with their children.

∽ COMPLETED HOMEWORK ∽

Week of _____

Homework checker this week is _____

Student name	Mon.	Tues.	Wed.	Thurs.	Fri.	Total

Walking Word Board

PURPOSE

It's important to provide children with a variety of ways for learning to spell. Not all children are comfortable risk takers, and they may be hesitant to use inventive spelling. And dictionaries may not be reasonable alternatives for young children. By offering options you can encourage children to use words from their oral vocabulary that they may not know how to spell, thereby increasing their written vocabulary.

A *walking* word board (so-called because we can easily take it with us wherever we are writing) not only helps children become more independent spellers but also builds a foundation for using dictionaries.

MATERIALS

- 2 foam core boards, 20" x 30" (check an art supply or picture-framing store)
- duct tape or other heavy, wide tape
- 26 library card pockets
- 26 index cards
- glue

HOW TO MAKE

1. Use heavy tape to connect the two pieces of foam core along one side so that they look like a big book and can easily free-stand on the floor.

2. Write each letter of the alphabet in large print on a library card pocket and at the top of an index card.

3. Evenly space and glue the pockets onto the foam core display. Place index cards in appropriate pockets.

HOW TO USE

1. A student who wants help spelling a word brings you the card from the pocket labeled with the first letter of the word.

2. You print the word and the student returns to his or her writing, replacing the card in the pocket after copying the word. It helps to number the words on each card. Then, if another child requests the same word, you can refer to the number.

REFLECTIONS

This approach to spelling gives all children, especially those who are not comfortable with inventive spelling, a chance to use "bigger" words. Children in my class automatically take the word board out when we begin any writing activity. As the year progresses, children often search the cards for words first (or ask a friend to help them search) before consulting me. They really see the board as a useful writing tool.

Take-Home Backpacks

∽ PURPOSE ∽

Children don't always have a chance to explore topics covered in class as much as they may want. To enable children to expand their knowledge about topics of interest, a colleague and I developed a series of take-home backpacks, complete with extended learning activities children can do at home with their parents. Take-home backbacks are an enjoyable way to create home-school bonds. And once made, backpacks require very little upkeep.

∽ MATERIALS ∽

- backpack
- a fiction book on the topic
- a nonfiction book on the topic
- journal
- sign-out sheet

∽ HOW TO MAKE ∽

1. Choose a topic, for example, birds.

2. Select a nonfiction book and a fiction book about birds.

3. In the journal or notebook, include the following:

- directions for using the backpack, including suggested activities and due date (see sample directions on page 43)
- blank copies of the Parent-Child Response Log (see reproducible on page 44)

4. Number each backpack to facilitate

record keeping (on the sign-out sheet, write the number next to the name of the student borrowing the backpack). Attach a luggage tag with your school address.

∞ HOW TO USE ∞

1. Let students take backpacks home for a predetermined amount of time, for example, from Wednesday to the following Monday, so that parents and children can use the backback over a weekend. This schedule also gives you a day's leeway before backpacks go home again to make sure all are in, complete, and ready to go.

2. Help keep your loss ratio low by having children and parents sign a contract before any backpacks go home that stresses the importance of returning all contents in good shape. (I include the contract in a Monday letter in which I explain the backpack program.)

3. Ask upper-grade students to help check each backpack in, making sure all the parts and pieces are included before it goes home with the next student.

∞ REFLECTIONS ∞

Take-home backpacks are very popular with both parents and children. Some of my students' parents even contribute new items to the backpacks. Many of our backpacks have curriculum-related themes. For example, one set stresses careers in science. Choosing themes that relate to the curriculum helps reinforce important concepts and deepen children's understandings. It's also a great way to involve parents in what their children are learning.

Sample Directions for Birds Activity Backpack

Dear Parents:

Please read this page before using any materials in this backpack!

This backpack contains books and activities about birds for you and your child to share. Please try to use the backpack each night during its stay in your home. The amount of time each night depends on your child's interest and attention and your other family needs.

Following are some ways you can use the materials in this backpack:

1. Give your child time to explore the backpack—to look at, feel, talk about, and experiment with the materials.

2. Read the books in the backpack:

Kids' First Book of Birdwatching
Beautiful Birds

3. Spend time together outside spotting birds. You'll find binoculars in the backpack. Use the Bird Watch Chart to keep track of birds you see.

4. Listen to the tape about birds.

5. Read and discuss some of the bird cards.

6. Use the birdseed in the pack to feed some birds. To make a bird feeder, apply peanut butter to the outside of the toilet paper tube and roll it in birdseed.

7. Complete the Parent-Child Response Log.

8. Check to make sure the following materials are in the backpack, then return by the date indicated for another child to borrow: 2 books, 2 binoculars, Bird Watch Chart, bird-watching tape, bird cards, jar of peanut butter, Parent-Child Response Log, and this journal.

(You may keep the birdseed and bird feeder.)

9. Date due _____

◯∽ PARENT-CHILD RESPONSE LOG ∽◯

Child's name: _____ This backpack is due back on: _____

PARENT AND CHILD:
Please tell what you used in the backpack together.

_____

_____

What was one of your favorite activities?

_____

_____

Can you think of an activity that you would like to add to this backpack?

_____

_____

CHILD:
Tell three new ideas you learned (either child or parent can do the writing).

1. _____

2. _____

3. _____

Is there something about this topic you would like to learn more about?

_____

PARENT AND CHILD:
How can you work together to learn more about this topic at home?

_____

_____

PARENT:
What are your feelings about using the materials in this backpack with your child? Please write comments and suggestions on the back of this paper.

44

Response Journal

⌘ PURPOSE ⌘

Children need to learn to apply, analyze, synthesize, and evaluate information, not just repeat knowledge to show comprehension. Fulfilling these needs requires a conscious effort on your part in all areas of literacy, including math. Careful questioning is one way to elicit higher-level thinking in oral responses. However, higher-level thinking in written expression is equally important. Response journals, although not new, need to be used with a stronger sense of purpose to encourage children to move beyond the lower levels of knowledge.

⌘ HOW TO USE ⌘

1. Each child needs a response journal. This can be a separate blank journal, a section in a notebook, or a section in an existing journal. Loose paper is not recommended. Having a special place to keep entries will help students see their responses as a collection of their thoughts throughout the entire year. And because response journals are also excellent evaluation sources, having students keep their entries in one place will make it easier for you to make use of this assessment information.

2. Before students begin writing in their journals, ask a question about a story you're reading. For example, with *Where the Wild Things Are* by Maurice Sendak (HarperCollins Children's Books), you might ask: "How would you feel if you were with Max that night?" Model a response that synthesizes what you read with how you would feel. With younger children begin by asking for information at the knowledge level. For example, ask students to list the characters in the story. Gradually move students to higher levels.

3. Once students get the general idea, ask another question and involve them in the modeling process.

4. When you feel students are ready to write their own responses, write a literature-related question on the overhead or chalkboard. Have students copy the question in their journals and then write a response after taking time to think and react.

5. Give students opportunities to share responses. For example, let small groups meet to discuss responses, or read them yourself and write notes back to students.

6. Remember that children have plateaus—as well as lows and highs—in learning, and that this will also occur in response journal writing. If this happens, be encouraging. Avoid "you can do better" types of responses to their work.

⌘ REFLECTIONS ⌘

A fellow teacher said that she "really gets to 'crawl' into a child's mind" when she reads response journals. Response journals can give you a clear picture of students' applied literacy at higher thinking levels—information we don't get from a steady diet of ditto sheets.

Keep in mind that working with response journals requires that you, too, work at higher levels of thinking than is required for lessons based on recall of facts. Be careful not to overdo using the journals nor to force these kinds of responses with every lesson. And remember that you need to model for students periodically if you expect them to continue to grow.

SECTION THREE

Literacy Empowerment: Teachers

Mini Literacy Diaries

⁓ PURPOSE ⁓

Letter grades on a ditto give a very small picture of a child's abilities in reading and language usage. It's in observing a child's everyday gains and plateaus that real learning growth is most evident. That's why keeping running comments about a child's literacy accomplishments can be such an effective assessment tool. I keep anecdotal records for each child on ringed index cards. They're small, easy to use, and, like a diary, they create a picture over time of a child's progress.

⁓ MATERIALS ⁓

- 4"x 6" lined index cards
- hole punch
- metal ring or a metal shower curtain ring

⁓ HOW TO MAKE ⁓

1. Write each child's name in the upper right corner of an index card.

2. Record information that is useful in meeting each child's needs. In the upper left corner, for example, record any special services the child receives, whether the child wears glasses or a hearing aid, and so on. I create codes for each type of information to simplify the process.

3. Punch holes in index cards and ring the student information card, along with 10 to 20 additional cards, through a metal ring to create a literacy diary for each child.

⁓ HOW TO USE ⁓

1. Have diaries handy as you work with children in individual or small or large group activities.

2. Record brief comments as you observe growth, concerns, or plateaus.

3. Date each comment and record a code letter to indicate the context of the entry, such as the following:

   J – journal observation
   S – small group observation
   I – individual oral reading
   L – oral language session

⁓ REFLECTIONS ⁓

It's easy to make mental notes about a child's progress but unrealistic to expect to be able to recall those observations weeks later during a parent conference or at report card time. These cards let me go back and review individual children's growth at any time. I use them to reevaluate and guide lesson plans or to conduct a conference. They are especially useful during the first month of school when I am trying to determine the best way to help each child reach his or her literacy potential.

Creating Materials Files

⌘ PURPOSE ⌘

Life in the classroom is too short to spend unnecessary time looking for ideas, materials, and resources you know you have (somewhere) to help teach a story, theme, or author focus. Because you no longer are turning to a single basal or textbook for teaching materials and plans, organization becomes an especially important factor in facilitating children's learning. If you organize from the beginning so that you can quickly retrieve materials, you'll eliminate needless frustrations, make better use of your resources, and, above all, grow as a facilitator.

⌘ MATERIALS ⌘

○ file cabinet
○ hanging file folders

⌘ HOW TO USE ⌘

1. Set up a file cabinet where you do most of your planning. I use hanging file folders because as they fill up with materials, they don't slide down in the drawer and become difficult to handle.

2. When you come across materials on a theme, author, or book that may be of value now or later, make copies and create a file. (Friends and I often share our files so I make duplicate copies.) Collect and file, for example, blackline masters, articles, and themed units from periodicals such as *Instructor* and *Creative Classroom*. I try to take the time to copy the materials when I see them. Otherwise, I probably won't remember where I saw them.

3. Continue to add to these files and create new ones as you gather more materials.

4. Keep a paper-size box on your desk so even when you can't get to your file cabinet right away, you can keep materials to be copied in one place. Take 10 to 15 minutes every once in a while to copy and file the materials you want to keep.

⌘ REFLECTIONS ⌘

This organization method has made planning so much easier for me. I feel myself growing in my ability to create richer literature environments for my students. As I return materials to the folders, I also file completed lesson plans. I never use exactly the same plan over again, because each group of children is different, but looking back on lessons lets me reflect on and adapt ideas that worked and also reminds me of those I need to scrap.

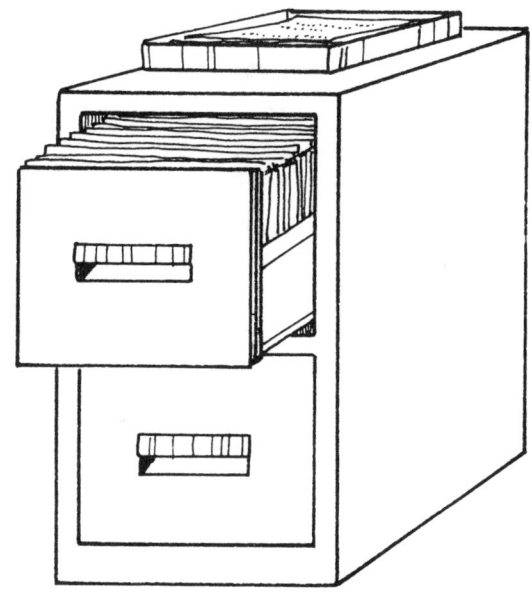

Find It Fast

∽ PURPOSE ∽

With each year of teaching come more and more teaching materials. I found it frustrating to begin a new theme knowing that I had related materials but unable to remember exactly where they were. Several years ago I began creating computer data bases for organizing classroom materials. For example, one data base lists by title and theme all of the books and tapes in the listening center. Instead of having to search through boxes and shelves to see what I have (or need) to develop a new theme, I check my data base and find out what's available at a glance.

∽ MATERIALS ∽

○ a software data base (I use Microsoft Works)

∽ HOW TO USE ∽

1. To organize information about listening center books and tapes

As you accumulate books and tapes for your listening center, add the information to a data base. Include book title and author, number of copies, theme or topic, and genre. (To make it even easier to find these materials when I need them, I keep books and tapes together in plastic bags.)

2. To organize information about sets of books

If you collect sets of books—for example, by using bonus points from student book clubs such as Scholastic See-Saw and Trumpet—it's helpful to know exactly what you've got in terms of titles, copies, themes, and so on. To provide quick access to this information, create a data base of book sets. Exchange copies of your data base with a colleague and double your resources.

3. To organize literature available through a building resource room

Our staff created a language resource room in our school that includes more than 150 different book sets. Each staff member has a data base list of what's available: book titles, theme areas, a range of appropriate grade level reading, the number of standard size or big book copies, read-along cassette tapes, and so on. A core level is designated for each title. If, for example, a book is designated a third grade core level book, any teacher in the third grade and above may use it but no class below third grade may use it for instructional purposes. This system helps ensure that students and teachers at each successive grade will have fresh literature for classroom use.

∽ REFLECTIONS ∽

I love teaching with a whole language philosophy, but because this approach requires considerable preparation time, I need to make sure I'm not spending unnecessary time hunting for materials. As I became more familiar with the opportunities for using computers to organize, I quickly learned how to make data bases. These systems enable me to store information in one place and, most importantly, to get it back very quickly without going through boxes and files.

A Ditto Alternative

∽ PURPOSE ∾

As you grow stronger in your whole-language-based philosophy, you'll continue to find ways to help children learn without relying on a mountain of ditto paper. But now and then, you may find that some area of the curriculum benefits from the drill that dittos can provide. Here's an alternative way to use dittos, without reverting to reams of paper.

∽ MATERIALS ∾

- workbooks or learning center source books
- copier that will enlarge to 18" x 24"
- laminator (optional)
- glue-backed magnetic tape
- magnetic chalkboard or a large piece of sheet metal (spray-paint the metal white to deflect shine and tape all edges)
- plastic bags for storage

∽ HOW TO USE ∾

1. Select activity or reproducible sheets that reinforce a concept or skill covered in class. Cut-and-paste activities lend themselves to this approach: they generally do not have a lot of type that would be difficult to see in a group setting, and children can take turns moving pieces to indicate their understanding or response.

2. Enlarge the worksheets to 18" x 24" and laminate them.

3. Cut apart any cut-and-paste activities. Adhere small pieces of glue-backed magnetic tape to the back of each piece.

4. Use the laminated cut-and-paste pieces on a magnetic surface for large or small group lessons.

5. Use other types of activities as you would a big book. Display the enlarged ditto paper, and let students volunteer responses as you work through the activity together. Or use the thumbs voting approach described on page 15 to monitor whole group responses.

6. For storage purposes, label a plastic food storage bag with the title and skill area of each sheet.

7. Record answers on the storage bags so that children can self-check answers.

∽ REFLECTIONS ∾

I like to use this activity because I get immediate feedback on students' understanding of concepts and skills, and I don't have to wait until I check their ditto papers later. I can also easily modify the activity to meet students' needs. For example, if I find that a few students need more instruction or clarification, I can move the activity to the side of a metal file cabinet (or use a metal sheet on the floor) for small group instruction.

Choosing and Using Literature

◎ PURPOSE ◎

Now that your literature selections are not bound by the next story in a basal, and you have the freedom to choose literature for your students, you'll want to make sure you are selecting the best and most appropriate books. Whether you choose stories to support a themed unit, for example, or to focus on a specific author, you must have a strong literary purpose for your selections.

◎ HOW TO DO ◎

1. Ask yourself some critical questions as you evaluate books for your students:

- Is the vocabulary appropriate?
- If students are emergent readers, does the book have strong elements of rhyme, rhythm, and repetition?
- Does the book have rich and colorful language that is also age appropriate?
- Will students be able to feel success with the book?

2. There are several ways to proceed.

- If you're developing a themed unit

Think about how your theme connects with the curriculum, and then look for books that support those connections. For example, if you're studying city transportation you can bring in social studies with a book on how transportation helps make a city work or physical science with a book about wheels and axles. Donald Crew's *Freight Train* (Morrow) and Gail Gibbons's *Trains* (Holiday House) are two that tie in.

- If you're doing an author study

Author studies are lots of fun because they let students delve into one person's writing styles, characterization, and illustrations. They also give children a chance to identify with authors as real people and encourage children to see themselves as authors, too.

- If you're building activities around one book

Because children are naturally drawn to storytelling, building activities around books makes sense. This is a good opportunity to introduce students to Caldecott medal and honor books. *Song and Dance Man* by Karen Ackerman (Knopf Books for Young Readers) is a yearly favorite with my students. In this charming story, Grandpa and his two grandchildren visit the attic, where Grandpa opens a trunk and takes the kids back in time. When we read this book, we talk about what being "old" means, draw pictures of ourselves as we'll look when we are old, and write about what we will do. We integrate math by graphing ages of older people in our families and use ages to discuss place value. In science we talk about how our bodies change as we grow older. Students further their understanding by reading with senior citizens at a retirement community. These activities create a stronger interest in the story and strengthen children's language abilities across the curriculum.

◎ REFLECTIONS ◎

Good books can do more than strengthen children's interest in literature. Carefully selected literature can foster children's language development and, in a broader sense, their understanding of the world around them. Good literature causes children to question, to ask why and what if. A good book makes children want to know more.

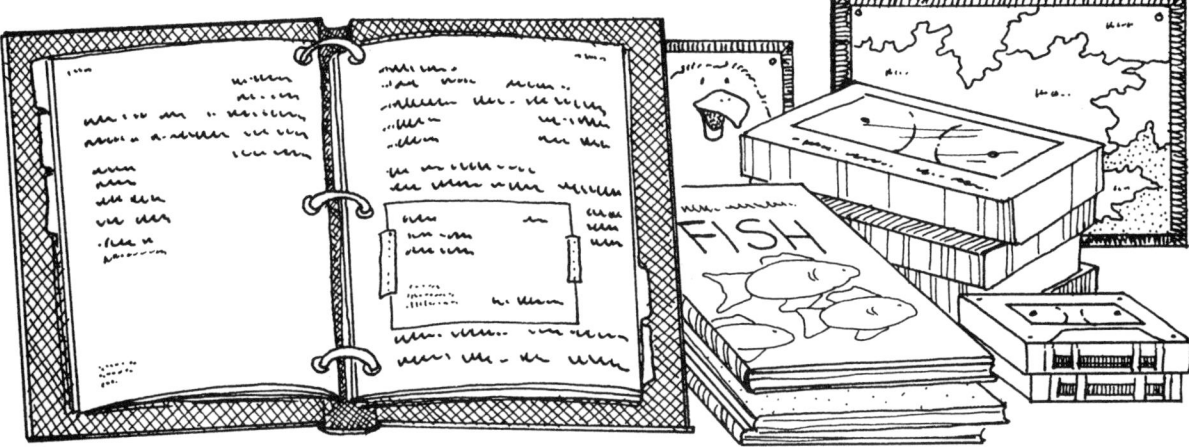

Resource Planning Book

∞ PURPOSE ∞

As you rely less and less on teacher guides for planning, you'll need to create a resource planning book that lists grade level objectives as identified by your state and/or school system and includes information on resources that you can use to meet those objectives and to provide a literacy-rich environment for your students.

∞ MATERIALS ∞

- three-ring binder
- notebook divider tabs

∞ HOW TO USE ∞

1. Create tab sections in the binder for different categories such as the following:

- grade level objectives
- word lists (for example, frequently used words in children's literature)
- library resources (special materials from school and public libraries, such as audiovisual materials)
- educational videos
- software
- bibliographies of content-related books (by subject or theme)
- community resources

2. Make copies of objectives, word lists, and so on, and place them in the appropriate sections. As you accumulate additional information, add it to the specific section.

3. As you prepare lessons, refer to the binder to quickly find out what related resources are available.

∞ REFLECTIONS ∞

It takes time to prepare a creative, strong, and vibrant literature lesson. But the time I spend is worth it to me if it means I don't have to use a teacher guide "recipe book" written by someone who doesn't know my students. With this binder, I don't waste any time gathering resources for these lessons. Another plus: by having information about building, district, and community resources at my fingertips, I'm much more likely to take advantage of them.

Teachers Helping Teachers

◌ PURPOSE ◌

It's no secret that cooperative learning is effective with students. Like students, teachers have a lot to gain by collaborating on a more regular basis. About once a month, teachers on our staff circulate a paper on which we write the literature-based themes or units we are weaving into our curriculum. This procedure enables us to share our resources and ideas with each other and promotes a feeling of cooperation schoolwide.

◌ MATERIALS ◌

○ Teachers Helping Teachers: Networking Sheet (see reproducible on page 55)

◌ HOW TO USE ◌

1. Create a master networking sheet by listing the names of participating teachers on a copy of the form on page 55.

2. About once a month, circulate a copy of the networking sheet.

3. After each teacher has had a chance to contribute, make and distribute copies for every teacher who participated. Rotate responsibility for this task by starting the circulation with a different teacher each month. Ask the last person to receive the sheet to make sure everyone gets a copy.

4. If you have materials on a topic another teacher is focusing on, offer to share ideas and materials. If you and another teacher are both focusing on the same topic, get together!

◌ REFLECTIONS ◌

This simple sheet has helped to break down the walls of isolation in our school and enabled a stronger curriculum dialogue to exist among staff members. We have also noticed that this networking tool has promoted interest in whole language and literature-based learning. Most of all, we're sharing great ideas instead of keeping them behind our classroom doors.

Teachers Helping Teachers

∽ NETWORKING SHEET ∽

In the area below your name, list units, themes, books, and authors that you and your students will be working with during _____. Please make sure that this paper
(month)
does not get stuck on your desk. It began circulating on _____ and should be back in the hands of the last person on the sheet by _____. This paper will then be duplicated and put in your mailbox.

Teacher:
What you're working on:

Teacher:
What you're working on:

Teacher:
What you're working on:

Teacher:
What you're working on:

Teacher:
What you're working on:

Teacher:
What you're working on:

Webbing a Lesson

∽ PURPOSE ∽

You are now the designer of your own literature program. Instead of using a teacher's guide that tells you what to do, you're deciding how you can use literature to integrate your curriculum and to create a strong, rich literature environment. You're like a spider, creating a web to capture your students' interest in a positive way. The best place to begin is by identifying a theme, author, or story as a focus. The next step is to build a web of possible integrative learning activities.

∽ MATERIALS ∽

○ webbing worksheet (see reproducible on page 57)

∽ HOW TO USE ∽

1. Keep in mind that quality, not quantity, is the key to building a web that successfully integrates your focus. You do not have to integrate all subject areas. Focus first on expanding students' language and higher thinking skills.

2. Start by writing your theme, author, or book title in the middle of the webbing worksheet. Let your imagination go wild with all the related ideas you can think of. Write them down in the appropriate subject sections. Set the paper aside several times and go back to it with fresh ideas.

3. When you feel you have exhausted your resources, review the ideas you have written down and highlight the best ones. Keep in mind that you do not need to generate an idea for each subject area. However, do consider and give priority to grade level objectives.

∽ REFLECTIONS ∽

I find that using a webbing approach to planning lessons helps the whole process flow more quickly than if I just try to develop an idea for each subject area. I file completed webbing worksheets for future use in my materials file (see page 49).

WEBBING WORKSHEET

- Social Studies
- Music-Movement
- Language Arts
- Science-Health
- Creative Writing
- Art
- Creative Thinking
- Math

SECTION FOUR

*Literacy Empowerment:
Parents and the Community*

Involving Parents

∽ PURPOSE ∽

It's so important to build bridges with students' parents. And research supports that when parents are involved, their children do better in school and beyond.

Get a head start on your home-school connections by sending a letter to the parents of your incoming students during the summer while they, like their children, have high hopes for a good and productive school year. Don't be shy about promoting your program. By hooking parents on your terrific classroom with this letter, you'll build parent interest and involvement right from the beginning of the year`.

∽ MATERIALS ∽

○ sample form letter (see pages 62–63)
○ student information form (see reproducibles on pages 64–65)
○ envelopes
○ postage

∽ HOW TO USE ∽

1. About a month before the beginning of a new school year, prepare a form letter to send to parents of all your new students. You might, for example, share information about the following:

- your philosophy and goals for the year
- what a day in your classroom is like
- the homework program
- ways other than dittos that parents can learn about their child's progress (by oral reading at home, by journal assignments, and so on)
- supplies students will need

2. Consider using this letter to invite parents and their children to an informal visit with you in the classroom. On that day I make sure there are plenty of books, activities, and computer programs for children to explore. While they're busy I have a chance to get to know their parents, to explain that I need them to be a part of our classroom, and to encourage them to volunteer, for example, by listening to students read.

3. Include a student information form with the letter for parents and children to complete together.

∽ REFLECTIONS ∽

Communicating with parents before a new school year starts helps make the first few days go more smoothly, especially for anxious children. These letters let parents know that their interest and support are valued. They get our partnership off to a quick start, which is the best thing for their children.

Sample Form Letter

Dear Parent,

Welcome to first grade at Portage Path School! Your child has been assigned to grow as a reader, writer, and mathematician in room 204 with me this school year. I am excited about spending the year with you and your child. I consider us a team—all three of us—in getting your child off to a good learning start in life. I would like to take the opportunity in this letter to give you some understanding and background that I feel you need to know before the first day of school. Please read the letter carefully.

This is my sixth year at Portage Path and my 24th year of teaching. I take my career in education very seriously and choose to spend many hours outside the classroom preparing instructional materials. I have a strong personal philosophy of education and feel you have the right to know what my foundation is for instruction in our room.

I believe that it is important to help develop each child into a strong learner. To accomplish this goal, children need to be guided in these areas:

1. Ownership: To motivate children to feel that they are learning because they want to, not because they have to please others.

2. Risk taking: All people have different levels of risk taking willingness. I will work hard to help children allow their curiosity and risk taking to be at their safe maximum so that they grow as self-starters in the learning process.

3. Flexibility: All children are not alike. I have a class of individual learners. It is important that I am always flexible with their emotional and intellectual growth.

You will find that I use many hands-on materials instead of ditto and worksheet pages, many children's literature books, computers, and many language and decision-making activities. Let me explain a little further. I have taken the state-required course objectives and the objectives of the CAT test that your child will take this spring and used them as my guidelines to sequence instructional skills. I have been using this method for four years. This year the entire school system is being trained in using this same method.

Using the objectives as a guide, I pull the best teaching ideas from many sources. I don't like to give dittos unless they are meaningful, so you will not be seeing many ditto sheets coming home. However, I will use other ways to let you know what we are doing in class and how your child is doing.

Every Monday your child will bring home a letter from me explaining what we will be working on that week and how you can help your child learn. I rarely skip a Monday so be sure to ask your child for the letter. Please feel free to contact me by note or phone if you have any concerns.

We have six computers in our classroom. Children will begin using computers the first day of school. Enclosed you will find a picture of a computer keyboard. This is for you and your child to practice where the keys are located. Start by calling out an alphabet letter and having your child try to locate it.

I firmly believe in parent involvement throughout the entire year. I would like for you to seriously consider volunteering in the classroom by listening to children read to you one-on-one. Volunteering will also give you an opportunity to observe our class.

Your child will need several supplies:
- backpack
- pair of scissors
- at least two pencils at all times
- glue stick
- old shirt to cover clothes during art projects

(I will supply crayons, a school box, and markers)

I ask that you make sure your child has breakfast every morning before school and gets a good night's sleep. I know the children will do better in school with this preparation. I will be available to meet you August 27 in room 204 between 1:00 and 2:00. Feel free to bring your child with you to check out the new room. If you come that day, please complete and bring the attached student information form.

We are a team, the three of us—you, your child, and me. Together we can have a warm, caring, and productive year. I am looking forward to meeting you and your child soon.

Sincerely,
Mrs. Karen Grindall

(side 1)

∽ STUDENT INFORMATION ∽

Child's name_____ Child's birth date_____

Mom_____ Address _____

Home phone_____ Work phone_____

Dad_____ Address _____

Home phone_____ Work phone_____

Other guardian_____ Address _____

Home phone_____ Work phone_____

What is the best time of day to call you regarding your child?_____

Are there any medical problems I should know about? _____

_____

_____

Are there any fears your child may have that I should know about? _____

_____

Parent volunteers are important in our classroom. Would you be willing to come into the room one hour a week to listen to a child read?_____

Are you available to volunteer: one hour a week_____ one hour a month_____ other_____?

Best day/time_____

What do you think are your child's strengths and weaknesses? _____

_____

_____

_____

_____

(side 2)

∽ ABOUT ME ∽

Please complete this side with your child.

Child's name _____ Date _____

How I look: _____

My family: _____
_____

My favorite thing to do is: _____

Sometimes I wish: _____
_____

I wish that people wouldn't: _____
_____

I have always wanted to visit: _____
_____

I am most afraid of: _____
_____

I like to collect: _____

I like to learn about: _____
_____

65

Weekly Letter to Parents

༄ PURPOSE ༄

Since I do not use or send home many duplicated papers, I feel that it is my responsibility to communicate with parents on a weekly basis so that they know what their child is learning in school. This communication helps strengthen the home-school connection and is particularly helpful to working parents who cannot make it into the classroom during the day.

༄ HOW TO MAKE ༄

1. After completing lesson plans for the week, type a letter to parents explaining what's going on in the classroom that week. You might include any of the following information:

- title and subject of literature you will be focusing on
- words you will be targeting in context and isolation
- objectives of math lessons for the week and how content areas such as science and social studies will be integrated
- a list of homework for the entire week
- ways parents can help their child become a stronger student
- a listing of events taking place in the classroom and school that week

2. Attach any permission slips for the week to this letter.

༄ REFLECTIONS ༄

As involved as children are in their learning during the day, it's just not realistic to expect them to go home every day and fill their parents in on what's going on in school. Weekly letters help maintain a communication line between home and school and give parents the information they need to guide their child through the week.

I send my letters home every Monday so that parents know when to expect them. It usually takes me about 10 minutes to type the letter and 3 minutes to make copies, and I consider the paper better used on this letter than on another ditto for the children. Parent feedback is overwhelmingly positive. I couldn't imagine not sending home a letter every Monday.

Parents As Reading Partners

◦ PURPOSE ◦

I feel that involving parents in their child's education is as important as guiding the child in learning. I make all attempts nonthreatening in order to get parents involved beyond the year that I spend with their child. Encouraging parents and children to read together through a classroom-based program is one of the ways I do this. I prepare book packages, complete with response sheets that ask parents to record their comments and observations. Children take the book packages home regularly as homework. The assignment not only promotes parent involvement in the child's schoolwork but also helps parents develop a better sense of how they can help their child learn.

◦ MATERIALS ◦

- literature books and student-made books from the classroom
- plastic storage bags
- Parent Response Sheet (see reproducible on page 68)
- book sign-out sheet (see reproducible on page 69)

◦ HOW TO USE ◦

1. Have children select books they feel comfortable reading.

2. Use book sign-out sheets to keep track of the books students borrow. Completed sign-out sheets go into each student's assessment file as a record of books read.

3. Send books and Parent Response Sheets home in plastic bags for homework that night.

4. When children return the book the next day (you might want to allow two days to make sure every child has a chance to read with a parent), check their names off on the sign-out sheets and collect the Parent Response Sheets.

◦ REFLECTIONS ◦

I read the Parent Response Sheets very carefully. Sometimes the comments give me clues to children's reading habits that I had not observed. This information helps me plan instruction that best meets the needs of each student. I keep the response sheets for the entire year and consider them an additional evaluation tool.

Comments sometimes signal parents' frustrations with their beginning readers. This information is just as important: it gives me an open door to call and explain how the reading process works and encourage parents to be supportive and patient with their young readers.

Finally, response sheets encourage parents to become stronger "kid watchers"—to be more aware of how their child reads and better able to foster literacy at home. This reading program sends a strong message that teaching and encouraging reading are not solely the responsibility of the school.

↜ PARENT RESPONSE SHEET ↝

Child's name_____ Date_____

Title of book read _____

Parent signature _____

Parent comments:

↜ PARENT RESPONSE SHEET ↝

Child's name_____ Date_____

Title of book read _____

Parent signature _____

Parent comments:

Books borrowed to take home by:

Date	Returned	Title

Listening Volunteers

∽ PURPOSE ∽

One of my ongoing goals is to have children read to an adult or older child as much as possible. I readily accept that there is no way humanly possible that I can listen to each student individually in a day, so I set up a program involving my richest resource—children's parents. At our orientation meeting in the summer (see sample form letter, page 62), I begin to recruit parents as volunteer listeners in the classroom.

∽ MATERIALS ∽

- a bulletin board display on which to record each child's reading progress (For example, cut out a balloon shape for each child; attach colorful ribbons or yarn; arrange and affix balloon shapes on bulletin board; write each child's name on a balloon. Children will attach a star to their balloons to indicate each book read.)
- Oral Reading Record for each child (see reproducible on page 74)
- pushpins
- monthly calendar
- Guidelines for Listening Volunteers and suggestions for reading strategies (see reproducibles on pages 72 and 73)
- parent sign-in book
- self-adhesive stars

∽ HOW TO MAKE ∽

1. Use bulletin board space easily accessible to children to design a display (as described above) for recording students' achievements in this read-aloud program.

2. Make an Oral Reading Record for each

child. I usually run these off on heavier stock colored paper. As children need a new sheet, I use a different color. That way, I can tell at a glance how far along they are. Place reading record sheets in a folder and tape to the bulletin board ledge or nearby wall space.

3. Place a container of pushpins near the bulletin board. Children will indicate they have books they are ready to read to a volunteer by placing a pushpin next to their name on the bulletin board.

4. Devise a system for recruiting parent volunteers. I send a letter home every Monday to let parents know what is going on in our classroom that week. At the end of the month, I also tell them that I need listening volunteers for the coming month. I attach a calendar of that month, marking days on which we have special assemblies, field trips, days off, guest speakers, and so on. I ask parents to sign their name on any other day that they can volunteer and return the calendar to school. I then make a master calendar and send it home with children whose parents volunteered, together with a copy of the Guidelines.

5. Create a sign-in book for volunteers. I keep track of volunteer hours and praise parents in the weekly letters. (We all like a little pat on the back—including parents!)

6. Create a special place for parents and children to read. For example, place a small table with two chairs near the bulletin board. Place a supply of pens and self-adhesive stars on the table.

HOW TO USE

1. Parent volunteers begin by listening to their own children read and then proceed by selecting children who have indicated they are ready to read by placing a pushpin next to their name on the bulletin board.

2. After a child has read to the volunteer, the parent completes the reading record sheet by filling in the date, book title, type of book read (trade book, big book, class-made book, or student-made book), and a brief, positive comment (how much you enjoyed the book, for example). Together, they put a self-adhesive star next to the entry for that day's book and on the bulletin board next to the child's name.

3. The child puts the record book and the reading record sheet away, and the parent selects another child to read by looking at the pushpins. To minimize disruptions, I have volunteers send the student who just finished to tap the next child.

REFLECTIONS

My students love reading to parent volunteers! I've been using parents as listening volunteers for four years. Though response to the program is often slow at first, children quickly sell the idea to more parents. By December, I usually have about half of the parents involved. And once I get parents in, I don't have any problem getting them to come back.

Most children read more than 100 books to parent volunteers over the course of a year. Their reading record sheets give me a clear picture of the types of literature students like to read and the level of difficulty they are selecting in their books for independent reading. Each child's sheet becomes another piece of my assessment package for that child.

The benefits of this program extend beyond the classroom. Many parents report that the experience encourages them to do more reading at home with their child. What a wonderful way to give children lots of practice and encouragement while providing an opportunity for parents to become more involved in their child's learning.

∽ GUIDELINES FOR LISTENING VOLUNTEERS ∽

1. When you come into the room, greet your child and hang up your coat.

2. Your child will meet you with a book at the table in the reading area.

3. Guide your child in reading the story aloud. See the attached sheet for suggestions on helping children use good reading strategies.

4. After your child has finished reading, fill in the Oral Reading Record. Under "Comments," you may want to say whether your child found the book easy or difficult, say that you had a great time, or make some other positive comment. Put a star next to the day's book in the space at the front of that line. You will find pens and stars on the table.

5. Give your child another star to put on the Listening Volunteers bulletin board. Check to see which children have a pushpin by their name (to indicate that they are ready to read a book to you). Have your child tap one of those children to read next.

6. The entire process starts all over again!

We really think you are special. Thanks for giving the children extra time. We need more people like you! If you are unable to make your scheduled time, I understand. But please call the office and let us know that you are not coming so your child will not become anxious.

◌ STRATEGIES A GOOD READER USES ◌

1. Skip over a word you don't know and come back to it later.

2. Use the pictures on the page if there are any.

3. Use the words around the unknown word to help give meaning.

4. Substitute another word or phrase.

5. Reread the sentence.

6. Read ahead to see if the next words or sentence gives meaning.

7. Attempt sounding it out, but don't forget the meaning of the words you have already read.

8. Try something else that might not be as difficult.

A good reader usually uses one of the first six strategies and relies on the last two only as a last resort.

ORAL READING RECORD

_____ has read these good books to a parent volunteer!

(star)	Date	Title	Type of Book	Comments

Tapping Community Resources

∞ PURPOSE ∞

Traditional field trips are not likely to have a place in your whole language classroom. Too often traditional field trips lack direct and specific links to learning opportunities and fail to actively involve children in learning experiences. However, by keeping an ongoing list of community resources you come across that relate to your curriculum, you can involve children in meaningful learning experiences and give them memories that last forever. Don't limit yourself to your current curriculum needs. Include ideas that might connect to a future unit, or even to another year and another class. Remember: even the most unlikely idea might prove realistic.

∞ MATERIALS ∞

- field trip idea sheet (a section in a notebook or appointment book that you usually have with you)
- section in Resource Planning Book (see page 53)

∞ HOW TO MAKE ∞

1. Idea sheets do not have to be neat and tidy. They should be a dumping space for all the ideas, unedited, that come to mind.

2. As an idea becomes more possible (you see an upcoming link to your curriculum or you get funding), use an idea worksheet to gather details and note possible literature and curriculum connections.

3. Keep idea worksheets in your Resource Planning Book in the community resources section.

4. Getting your field trip off the ground is up to you, but having a clear idea of how the trip can help integrate your curriculum and enhance learning can only help secure necessary approval and, possibly, funding.

∞ REFLECTIONS ∞

Imagine the impression a close-up 35-ton crane makes on a group of six-year-olds! One of our most memorable field trips was to a local crane company where workers demonstrated how a crane works and explained how they use math and reading in their jobs.

Many teachers are timid about asking people in the community to get involved. But once you start asking you will find very few people will turn you down, as long as your request is reasonable and the safety of the children is ensured. Getting involved is good public relations for them (they do, after all, have something at stake in the education of future employees) and good public relations for the school.

Parent Backpacks

✤ PURPOSE ✤

Research clearly supports a connection between parent involvement and student success. And confidence in the role of parent is an important foundation for guiding and encouraging children at home. When a parent's self-esteem about this role is high, this is apt to set the stage for stronger self-esteem in the child and success in school and beyond. Book backpacks are a way to invite parents to read books and articles that can enhance their parenting skills and help them create positive environments for learning at home.

✤ MATERIALS ✤

- a collection of parenting books, articles, and videos, including some with ideas on parenting and others on activities for parents to do with children (see reproducible on page 77 for recommended titles)
- letter to parents, including a list of available materials
- request form
- backpacks for the materials to go to and from school safely
- sign-out sheet

✤ HOW TO USE ✤

1. In a letter to parents, explain how the book-backpack lending system works. Include an annotated list of available materials, noting, for example, books on parenting issues, on ages and stages, and on activities for stimulating children's learning at home.

2. Attach a request form to the letter. Have parents indicate their first through fifth choices of materials and sign to accept responsibility for materials borrowed. Indicate the date the backpack should be returned. Leave a space for comments, and encourage parents to suggest other items they would like included in the lending program.

3. Pack up the materials requested and send the backpack home with the child. Note on the sign-out sheet the parent's name, date, materials borrowed, and the date they're expected back.

✤ REFLECTIONS ✤

I acquired my parenting materials through several small school district and local foundation grants. In addition to seeking grants, you might ask your PTA to donate materials, or invite a local bookstore to become your parent backpack partner.

My first backpacks included some very basic parenting books as well as books that helped explain the whole language philosophy that I embrace. As time went on I added books with activities for helping children learn at home. Most recently I find that I am lending more professional books.

I've begun to realize that lending parenting books is like making a batch of cookies. The smell of cookies baking makes us want to sample them fresh from the oven. For some parents, reading the more basic books makes them want to read more. Last summer I loaned three of my newest professional books to parents and really enjoyed our conversations after they finished reading them. Parents are our partners in their children's education—why not build bridges instead of barriers?

RECOMMENDED TITLES

BOOKS ON PARENTING SKILLS

You're a Better Parent Than You Think!
  by Raymond N. Guarendi (Prentice Hall)

Back to the Family
  by Raymond N. Guarendi (Simon & Schuster)

How to Develop Your Children's Creativity
  by Reynold Bean (Price Stern Sloan)

The Measure of Our Success
  by Marian Wright Edelman (Beacon Press)

WHOLE LANGUAGE BOOKS

I Learn to Read and Write the Way I Learn to Talk
  by Marlene Barron (Richard C. Owen Publishers)

What's Whole in Whole Language?
  by Kenneth S. Goodman (Scholastic)

HOME LEARNING ACTIVITIES

Prime Time Together... with Kids
  by Donna Erickson (Augsburg Fortress Publishers)

More Prime Time Activities with Kids
  by Donna Erickson (Augsburg Fortress Publishers)

1001 Ways to Improve Your Child's Schoolwork
  by Lawrence J. Greene (Dell)

MegaSkills: How Families Help Children Succeed in School and Beyond
  by Dorothy Rich (Houghton Mifflin)

365 TV-Free Activities You Can Do with Your Child
  by Steve Bennett & Ruth Bennett (Bob Adams)

Is Your Bed Still There When You Close the Door?
  by Jane M. Healey (Doubleday)

Games for Reading
  by Peggy Kaye (Pantheon Books)

VIDEOS

Back to the Family by Raymond N. Guarendi

The Self-Confident Parent by Raymond N. Guarendi

(Videos available at The Company of Kids, 80 West Center Street, Akron, OH 44308)

Literacy Heroes

⟗ PURPOSE ⟗

I read to my students frequently during the school day. But to help students develop a strong sense of why reading is important in all walks of life, I turn to prominent citizens whom the children might recognize and ask them to become Literacy Heroes for my first graders.

⟗ MATERIALS ⟗

- a list of possible guest readers
- sample invitation (see reproducible on page 79)
- stationery and postage for letters and return postcards

⟗ HOW TO USE ⟗

1. Write letters inviting prominent, successful community people to your classroom to read a book to the students. Include a return postcard for their responses. I ask Literacy Heroes to stop by a local children's bookstore to purchase a copy of a favorite book they would like to share with my budding readers, and then donate to the class library.

2. Have the guest reader read the book aloud and then talk about reading. For example, the guest reader might talk about what he or she remembers about being a beginning reader or why he or she is really happy to be a good reader.

3. Invite the guest reader to listen to a few children read aloud at the reading center. Before your guest says good-bye, ask each guest reader to write a note to the children in the book, then place it in a special section of the classroom library.

⟗ REFLECTIONS ⟗

This program not only benefits the children, but it also enables people from the community to obtain a better picture of today's classrooms. Children develop special appreciation for the wonderful books our Literacy Heroes donate and are often inspired by these books to read others by the same author.

This year I extended the program to involve outstanding minority high school students. A small grant let me set up an account at a local children's bookstore to cover the cost of books that the high school students choose to read and donate.

Feedback from our Literacy Heroes is extremely positive. In fact, many of our guest readers recommend other people they work with who want to participate. This program provides children with real heroes—doctors, educators, well-known personalities, outstanding high school students, and hardworking business people—all letting my students know that literacy is important.

Dear _____,

Students in our class are working very hard to become reading and writing literate. I would like to invite you to help by becoming part of a new program called Literacy Heroes. Here's how the program works.

You go to the children's section of a local bookstore and purchase a book that you would like to share with my students. On a prearranged date, you visit our classroom and read the book to the class. Inside the book you write a note to students about the importance of reading and leave the book as a gift to the children in our classroom library. You then stay an extra half hour to listen to some of the children read one-on-one with you.

My students read and write every day. However, they need to hear from other people—not just their classroom teacher—that reading and writing are very important. Enclosed you will find a postcard for your response. If you are interested please select a date between _____ and _____. We would like to have you visit us on that date at ___:00. Please include a daytime and evening phone number so that I can reach you to confirm the date.

I appreciate your willingness to help the next generation of leaders become literate readers and writers. They need your good example now! If you have any questions, please contact me at _____.

Sincerely,

Open-Door Friends

∞ PURPOSE ∞

In my community, just like yours, we have elderly neighbors who have so much to give. Several years ago I began to actively recruit senior citizens to work with my students. I found their warmth and love formed a natural learning bridge across the generations. The difference between this and other volunteer programs is the open-door policy. Rather than limit these volunteers by a schedule, I invite them to visit at their convenience. My students benefit both from the spontaneity of the arrangement and from having volunteers who visit when they feel their best.

∞ HOW TO USE ∞

1. Recruit volunteers. I started out by writing a small "I need some senior citizens to listen to my students read" article in a neighborhood newspaper. From that article I found three wonderful ladies who were interested in "trying it out."

2. Invite prospective volunteers to visit after school for an information session. I emphasize that I want them to first volunteer on a trial basis. If they enjoy the experience, we'd love to have them become a part of our classroom family. I also let them know that if they are not comfortable with volunteering, I understand, and they can feel free to not continue. This understanding leaves the options open in a nonthreatening way.

3. Give volunteers a copy of your daily schedule and a calendar of special dates (school closings, assemblies, field trips, and so on). I let volunteers know my door is wide open: they may visit at their convenience.

4. Prepare children for the volunteers who will become their friends by sharing literature about older people, for example:

How Does It Feel to Be Old?
by Norma Farber
(Dutton Children's Books)

Music, Music for Everyone
by Vera B. Williams
(Morrow)

Talk about grandparents and what it is like to get older. Make a class book about older friends. Have each child tell about a special older friend. Work to build a sense of trust and understanding in children before the seniors begin volunteering.

5. Decide how senior volunteers can best help in your classroom. I have them follow the same procedures as in the Listening Volunteers program (see page 70).

∞ REFLECTIONS ∞

When I first started this program, I did it to help the children but quickly realized that it served another purpose as well—helping senior citizens feel purposeful. The children absolutely love having them in the room.

Two years ago I expanded this project to include a retirement community near our school. We began by visiting and reading with 20 seniors who became our very dear friends. With the assistance of a Crossroads Grant from Apple Corporation, we were able to place a computer and modem at the facility and train several seniors in using the equipment. We have the same equipment in our classroom. Now my students and their new friends write notes back and forth using telecommunications. This project shows intergenerational learning at its best!